Fighting for
Holiness

The Crossway Short Classics Series

The Emotional Life of Our Lord

B. B. WARFIELD

Encouragement for the Depressed

CHARLES SPURGEON

The Expulsive Power of a New Affection

THOMAS CHALMERS

Fighting for Holiness

J. C. RYLE

The Freedom of a Christian: A New Translation

MARTIN LUTHER

Heaven Is a World of Love
JONATHAN EDWARDS

The Life of God in the Soul of Man
HENRY SCOUGAL

The Lord's Work in the Lord's Way and No Little People
FRANCIS A. SCHAEFFER

Selected Sermons
LEMUEL HAYNES

What Did the Cross Achieve?
J. I. PACKER

FIGHTING

FOR

HOLINESS

J. C. RYLE

WHEATON, ILLINOIS

Fighting for Holiness

Copyright © 2022 by Crossway

Published by Crossway
    1300 Crescent Street
    Wheaton, Illinois 60187

Cover design: Jordan Singer

Cover image: "Blackthorn" by William Morris. (Bridgeman Images)

First printing 2022

Printed in China

Scripture quotations in the text are from sources not identified by the author.

Trade paperback ISBN: 978-1-4335-8008-6
ePub ISBN: 978-1-4335-8011-6
PDF ISBN: 978-1-4335-8009-3
Mobipocket ISBN: 978-1-4335-8010-9

Library of Congress Cataloging-in-Publication Data

Names: Ryle, J. C. (John Charles), 1816–1900, author.
Title: Fighting for holiness / J.C. Ryle.
Description: Wheaton, Illinois: Crossway, 2022. | Series: Crossway short classics | Includes bibliographical references and index.
Identifiers: LCCN 2021020257 (print) | LCCN 2021020258 (ebook) | ISBN 9781433580086 (trade paperback) | ISBN 9781433580093 (pdf) | ISBN 9781433580109 (mobi) | ISBN 9781433580116 (epub)
Subjects: LCSH: Holiness. | Christian life.
Classification: LCC BT767 .R9495 2022 (print) | LCC BT767 (ebook) | DDC 234/.8—dc23
LC record available at https://lccn.loc.gov/2021020257
LC ebook record available at https://lccn.loc.gov/2021020258

Crossway is a publishing ministry of Good News Publishers.

RRDS 34 33 32 31 30 29 28 27 26 25 24
   14 13 12 11 10 9 8 7 6 5 4 3 2

Contents

Foreword

THIS LITTLE TRACT was originally published under the title *Are You Fighting?* John Ryle, the most popular evangelical tract writer of his generation, knew how to grab his readers' attention. His exhortations are direct, vigorous, personal, and practical. Many of his tracts carry similar pithy titles, designed to startle us and wake us up: *Are You Forgiven?*, *Are You Happy?*, *Are You Holy?*, *Do You Believe?*, *Are You Free?*, *Do You Love Christ?*, *Repent or Perish!*

Are You Fighting? was written in December 1870, when armed conflict between Prussia and France was engulfing continental Europe. French forces were starved into submission in the Siege of Metz and routed at the Battle of Sedan. Napoleon III, *Empereur des Français*, was captured and deposed, and German troops encircled Paris. The British government maintained a studied neutrality, but the newspapers were filled every day with dramatic reports from across the English Channel. It presaged the Great War of the next generation. As Ryle wrote in his tract,

> We meet each other at a critical period of the world's history. Men's minds are full of "wars and rumours of wars". Men's hearts are full of fear while they look at the things which seem coming on the earth. On every side the horizon looks black and gloomy. Who can tell when the storm will burst?[1]

1   J. C. Ryle, *Are You Fighting? A Question for 1871. Being Thoughts on 1 Timothy vi. 12* (London: William Hunt, 1871), 4.

But Ryle saw the opportunity to drive home a spiritual lesson. The Franco-Prussian War was the preacher's hook to lay hold of an audience and challenge them about fighting the Christian war. His tract was designed to be highly engaging, and easy to give away to friends and neighbors, sold in bulk at two shillings per dozen.

Ryle's writing has an urgent, evangelistic heartbeat. He pleads with us to take seriously the pursuit of holiness. In an age when the character and conduct of Christians are often indistinguishable from the secular world—as endemic today as in the 1870s—it is an appeal we desperately need to hear. Worldliness has crept into the church. Many professing Christians, in Ryle's words, succumb to a life of "religious ease" with no desire to wrestle in prayer or fight against temptation. Too often, our spiritual lives are marked by "apathy, stagnation, deadness, and indifference." This tract is a call to arms. Ryle exhorts us to take action: "Shake off your past carelessness and unbelief. Come out from the ways of a thoughtless, unreasoning world. Take up the cross, and become a good soldier of Christ."

Ryle's primary target is the half-hearted Christian, who has no ambition to live differently from the rest of the world, or to be more holy this year than last. But he also has a second target in mind: the passivist Christian (or, in the context of spiritual warfare, the "pacifist" Christian) who has laid down their arms and foolishly thinks that godliness is automatic. In the 1870s, a new group of teachers rose to prominence in the Victorian Church, promoting holiness without effort. They advocated the "higher Christian life," which emphasized resting and abiding in place of struggling and striving. One of the most popular holiness manuals was *The Christian's Secret of a*

Happy Life (1875) by Pennsylvanian author Hannah Whitall Smith, who taught that it was as silly to urge a Christian to grow in holiness as to urge a child to grow in height. Conscious effort was unnecessary and even counterproductive. Christians should simply yield themselves to God, without fighting against sin, and let the Holy Spirit do the sanctifying work single-handedly. Smith and her husband toured Britain, teaching these passivist doctrines, which took root at Bible conventions like Keswick in the Lake District. These ideas gave birth to mottos like "Let go and let God" and "Don't wrestle, just nestle."

Ryle argued that this new approach to holiness was ignoring half the Bible. The New Testament epistles, for example, often urge us to strive for practical holiness by holding our tongues, keeping our tempers, watching our steps, guarding our relationships, resisting the devil. The "higher life" advocates claimed that the active struggles against sin pictured in Romans 7 are those of a law-bound moralist, not a Spirit-filled Christian, but Ryle retorted that "the greatest divines in every age since the Reformation have steadily and continuously maintained, that it is a literal, perfect, accurate, correct photograph of the experience of every true saint of God."[2] Sanctity requires daily struggle. No one becomes holy by accident. Ryle therefore collected a few of his tracts into a single volume, *Holiness* (1877), his most famous publication. He retooled *Are You Fighting?* for this new purpose, adding some extra flourishes to drive his point home. Scattered throughout this new edition are direct rebuttals of the "higher life" teachers:

2   J. C. Ryle in *The Record* newspaper, May 28, 1875.

He that would understand the nature of true holiness must know that the Christian is a "man of war." If we would be holy, we must fight.

He that pretends to condemn "fighting" and teaches that we ought to sit still and "yield ourselves to God" appears to me to misunderstand his Bible, and to make a great mistake.

Where there is grace, there will be conflict. The believer is a soldier. There is no holiness without a warfare. Saved souls will always be found to have fought a fight.

May we never forget that without fighting there can be no holiness while we live, and no crown of glory when we die!

The worldly Christian and the passivist Christian make the same mistake. They both fail to take seriously the repeated commands of Scripture to keep fighting for personal holiness, under the banner of Christ, with the Holy Spirit as our strong ally. Ryle's invigorating tract is a deep challenge and a warm-hearted encouragement to pursue godliness with all our energies, to the very end of our days.

Andrew Atherstone
Latimer Research Fellow, Wycliffe Hall
University of Oxford

Series Preface

JOHN PIPER ONCE WROTE that books do not change people, but paragraphs do. This pithy statement gets close to the idea at the heart of the Crossway Short Classics series: some of the greatest and most powerful Christian messages are also some of the shortest and most accessible. The broad stream of confessional Christianity contains an astonishing wealth of timeless sermons, essays, lectures, and other short pieces of writing. These pieces have challenged, inspired, and borne fruit in the lives of millions of believers across church history and around the globe.

The Crossway Short Classics series seeks to serve two purposes. First, it aims to beautifully preserve these short historic pieces of writing through new high-quality physical editions. Second, it aims to transmit them to a new generation of readers, especially readers who may not be inclined or able to access a larger volume. Short-form content is especially valuable today, as the challenge of focusing in a distracting, constantly moving world becomes more intense. The volumes in the Short Classics series present incisive, gospel-centered grace and truth through a concise, memorable medium. By connecting readers with these accessible works, the Short Classics series hopes to introduce Christians to those great heroes of the faith who wrote them, providing readers with representative works that both nourish the soul and inspire further study.

Readers should note that the spelling and punctuation of these works have been lightly updated where applicable. Scripture references and other citations have also been added where appropriate. Language that reflects a work's origin as a sermon or public address has been retained. Our goal is to preserve as much as possible the authentic text of these classic works.

Our prayer is that the Holy Spirit will use these short works to arrest your attention, preach the gospel to your soul, and motivate you to continue exploring the treasure chest of church history, to the praise and glory of God in Christ.

Biography of J. C. Ryle

JOHN CHARLES RYLE (1816–1900) was born in England and educated at Oxford University. At one point, he aspired to a career in politics but was unable to pursue this due to financial difficulties. Instead, Ryle pursued a career in ministry in the Church of England. His plain, passionate style and emphasis on Scripture earned him a reputation as a dynamic minister.

Ryle authored many books and tracts, but his most popular and famous work is probably *Holiness: Its Nature, Hindrances, Difficulties, and Roots*, published in 1877. Ryle was concerned that many Christians in his day had grown indifferent toward practical matters of faithfulness and purity. In a Puritan-like style, Ryle challenged his readers by reminding them of the great importance the Bible places on personal holiness. "The immense importance," Ryle wrote, "of 'adorning the doctrine of God our Saviour' and making it lovely and beautiful by our daily habits and tempers has been far too much overlooked."[1]

Ryle expressed this emphasis on the transformative effects of the gospel with books such as *Thoughts for Young Men* and *Practical Religion*. Throughout his ministry, Ryle sought to bring together both belief and behavior by showing how the same Christ whom believers confess with their mouths also creates a new heart in everyone who is born again. In 1880, Ryle was appointed the first bishop of Liverpool, a position he held until his retirement shortly before his death in 1900.

---

1   J. C. Ryle, *Holiness: Its Nature, Hindrances, Difficulties, and Roots* (Durham: Evangelical Press, 1979), xvii.

FIGHTING

FOR

HOLINESS

Fight the good fight of faith.

1 Timothy 6:12

IT IS A CURIOUS FACT that there is no subject about which most people feel such deep interest as "fighting." Young men and maidens, old men and little children, high and low, rich and poor, learned and unlearned all feel a deep interest in wars, battles, and fighting.

This is a simple fact, whatever way we may try to explain it. We should call that Englishman a dull fellow who cared nothing about the story of Waterloo or Inkerman or Balaclava or Lucknow. We should think that heart cold and stupid that was not moved and thrilled by the struggles at Sedan and Strasburg and Metz and Paris during the war between France and Germany.

But there is another warfare of far greater importance than any war that was ever waged by man. It is a warfare that concerns not two or three nations only but every Christian man and woman born into the world. The warfare I speak of is the spiritual warfare. It is the fight that everyone who would be saved must fight about his soul.

This warfare, I am aware, is a thing of which many know nothing. Talk to them about it, and they are ready to set you down as a madman, an enthusiast, or a fool. And yet it is as real and true as any war the world has ever seen. It has its hand-to-hand conflicts and its wounds. It has its watchings and fatigues. It has its sieges and assaults. It has its victories and its defeats. Above all, it has consequences that are awful, tremendous, and most peculiar. In earthly warfare, the consequences to nations are often temporary and remediable. In the spiritual warfare, it is very different. Of that warfare, the consequences, when the fight is over, are unchangeable and eternal. It is of this warfare that St. Paul spoke to Timothy when he wrote those burning words, "Fight the good fight of faith; lay hold on eternal life."

It is of this warfare that I propose to speak in this paper. I hold the subject to be closely connected with that of sanctification and holiness. He that would understand the nature of true holiness must know that the Christian is "a man of war." If we would be holy, we must fight.

I

The first thing I have to say is this: true Christianity is a fight.

True Christianity! Let us mind that word "true." There is a vast quantity of religion current in the world that is not true, genuine

Christianity. It passes muster; it satisfies sleepy consciences; but it is not good money. It is not the real, that which was called Christianity eighteen hundred years ago. There are thousands of men and women who go to churches and chapels every Sunday, and call themselves Christians. Their names are in the baptismal register. They are reckoned Christians while they live. They are married with a Christian marriage service. They mean to be buried as Christians when they die. But you never see any "fight" about their religion! Of spiritual strife and exertion and conflict and self-denial and watching and warring, they know literally nothing at all. Such Christianity may satisfy man, and those who say anything against it may be thought very hard and uncharitable, but it certainly is not the Christianity of the Bible. It is not the religion that the Lord Jesus founded and his apostles preached. It is not the religion that produces real holiness. True Christianity is "a fight."

The true Christian is called to be a soldier, and must behave as such from the day of his conversion to the day of his death. He is not meant to live a life of religious ease, indolence, and security. He must never imagine for a moment that he can sleep and doze along the way to heaven, like one traveling in an easy carriage. If he takes his standard of Christianity from the children of this world, he may be content with such notions, but he will find no countenance for them in the word of God. If the Bible is the rule of his faith and practice, he will find his course laid down very plainly in this matter. He must "fight."

With whom is the Christian soldier meant to fight? Not with other Christians. Wretched indeed is that man's idea of religion who fancies that it consists in perpetual controversy! He who is never satisfied unless he is engaged in some strife between church and church, chapel and chapel, sect and sect, faction and faction, party and party knows nothing yet as he ought to know. No doubt, it may be absolutely needful sometimes to appeal to law courts, in order to ascertain the right interpretation of a church's articles and rubrics and formularies. But, as a general rule, the cause of sin is never so much helped as when Christians waste their strength in quarreling with one another and spend their time in petty squabbles.

No, indeed! The principal fight of the Christian is with the world, the flesh, and the devil. These are his never-dying foes. These are the three chief enemies against whom he must wage war. Unless he gets the victory over these three, all other victories are useless and vain. If he had a nature like an angel, and were not a fallen creature, the warfare would not be so essential. But with a corrupt heart, a busy devil, and an ensnaring world, he must either "fight" or be lost.

He must fight *the flesh*. Even after conversion, he carries within him a nature prone to evil, and a heart weak and unstable as water. That heart will never be free from imperfection in this world, and it is a miserable delusion to expect it. To keep that heart from going astray, the Lord Jesus bids us "watch and pray." The spirit may be ready, but the flesh is weak. There is need of a daily struggle and a daily wrestling in prayer. "I keep under my body," cries St. Paul, "and bring it into subjection." "I see a law in my members warring against the law of my mind, and bringing me into captivity." "O wretched man that I am, who shall deliver me from the body of this death?" "They that are Christ's have crucified the flesh with the affections and lusts." "Mortify your members which are upon the earth." (Mark 14:38; 1 Cor. 9:27; Rom. 7:23, 24; Gal. 5:24; Col. 3:5)

He must fight *the world*. The subtle influence of that mighty enemy must be daily resisted, and without a daily battle can never be overcome. The love of the world's good things, the fear of the world's laughter or blame, the secret desire to keep in with the world, the secret wish to do as others in the world do, and not to run into extremes—all these are spiritual foes that beset the Christian continually on his way to heaven and must be conquered. "The friendship of the world is enmity with God: whosoever therefore will be a friend of the world is the enemy of God." "If any man love the world, the love of the Father is not in him." "The world is crucified to me, and I unto the world." "Whatsoever is born of God overcometh the world." "Be not conformed to this world." (James 4:4; 1 John 2:15; Gal. 6:14; 1 John 5:4; Rom. 12:2)

He must fight *the devil*. That old enemy of mankind is not dead. Ever since the fall of Adam and Eve, he has been "going to and fro in the earth, and walking up and down in it," and striving to compass one great end: the ruin of man's soul. Never slumbering and never sleeping, he is always "going about as a lion seeking whom he may devour." An unseen enemy, he is always near us, about our path and about our bed, and spying out all our ways. A "murderer and a liar" from the beginning, he labors night and day to cast us down to hell. Sometimes by leading into superstition, sometimes by suggesting infidelity, sometimes by one kind of tactics, and sometimes by another, he is always carrying on a campaign against our souls. "Satan hath desired to have you, that he may sift you as wheat." This mighty adversary must be daily resisted if we wish to be saved. But "this kind goeth not out" but by watching and praying, and fighting, and putting on the whole armor of God. The strong man armed will never be kept out of our hearts without a daily battle. (Job 1:7; 1 Pet. 5:8; John 8:44; Luke 22:31; Eph. 6:11)

Some men may think these statements too strong. You fancy that I am going too far and laying on the colors too thickly. You are secretly saying to yourself that men and women in England may surely get to heaven without all this trouble and warfare and fighting. Listen to me for a few minutes, and I will show you that I have something to say on God's behalf.

Remember the maxim of the wisest general that ever lived in England: "In time of war it is the worst mistake to underrate your enemy, and try to make a little war." This Christian warfare is no light matter. Give me your attention and consider what I say.

What saith the Scripture? "Fight the good fight of faith, lay hold on eternal life." "Endure hardness, as a good soldier of Jesus Christ." "Put on the whole armour of God, that ye may be able to stand against the wiles of the devil. For we wrestle not against flesh and blood, but against principalities, against powers, against the ruler of the darkness of this world, against spiritual wickedness in high places. Wherefore take unto you the whole armour of God, that you may be able to withstand in the evil day, and having done all to stand." "Strive to enter in at the strait gate." "Labour for the meat that endureth unto everlasting life." "Think not that I came to send peace on the earth: I came not to send peace but a sword." "He that hath no sword let him sell his garment and buy one." "Watch ye, stand fast in the faith:

quit you like men, be strong." "War a good warfare, holding faith and a good conscience." (1 Tim. 6:12; 2 Tim. 2:3; Eph. 6:11–13; Luke 13:24; John 6:27; Matt. 10:34; Luke 22:36; 1 Cor. 16:13; 1 Tim. 1:18, 19)

Words such as these appear to me clear, plain, and unmistakable. They all teach one and the same great lesson, if we are willing to receive it. That lesson is that true Christianity is a struggle, a fight, and a warfare. He that pretends to condemn "fighting" and teaches that we ought to sit still and "yield ourselves to God" appears to me to misunderstand his Bible, and to make a great mistake.

What says the baptismal service of the Church of England? No doubt, that service is uninspired, and, like every uninspired composition, it has its defects; but to the millions of people all over the globe, who profess and call themselves English churchmen, its voice ought to speak with some weight. And what does it say? It tells us that over every new member who is admitted into the Church of England the following words are used: "I baptize thee in the name of the Father, the Son, and the Holy Ghost." "I sign this child with the sign of the cross, in token that hereafter he shall not be ashamed to confess the faith of Christ crucified, and manfully *to fight* under His banner against sin, the world, and the devil, and to continue Christ's faithful soldier and servant unto his life's end."

Of course, we all know that in myriads of cases baptism is a mere form, and that parents bring their children to the font without faith or prayer or thought, and consequently receive no blessing. The man who supposes that baptism in such cases acts mechanically, like a medicine, and that godly and ungodly, praying and prayerless parents, all alike get the same benefit for their children must be in a strange state of mind. But one thing, at any rate, is very certain. Every baptized churchman is by his profession a "soldier of Jesus Christ," and is pledged "to fight under His banner against sin, the world, and the devil." He that doubts it had better take up his prayer book and read, mark, and learn its contents. The worst thing about many very zealous churchmen is their total ignorance of what their own prayer book contains.

Whether we are churchmen or not, one thing is certain: this Christian warfare is a great reality, and a subject of vast importance. It is not a matter like church government and ceremonial, about which men may differ, and yet reach heaven at last. Necessity is laid upon us. We must fight. There are no promises in the Lord Jesus Christ's Epistles to the Seven Churches, except to those who "overcome." Where there is grace, there will be conflict. The believer is a soldier. There is no holiness without a warfare. Saved souls will always be found to have fought a fight.

It is a fight of *absolute necessity*. Let us not think that in this war we can remain neutral and sit still. Such a line of action may be possible in the strife of nations, but it is utterly impossible in that conflict that concerns the soul. The boasted policy of noninterference, the "masterly inactivity" pleases so many statesmen, the plan of keeping quiet and letting things alone—all this will never do in the Christian warfare. Here, at any rate, no one can escape serving under the plea that he is "a man of peace." To be at peace with the world, the flesh, and the devil is to be at enmity with God, and in the broad way that leadeth to destruction. We have no choice or option. We must either fight or be lost.

It is a fight of *universal necessity*. No rank or class or age can plead exemption, or escape the battle.

Ministers and people, preachers and hearers, old and young, high and low, rich and poor, gentle and simple, kings and subjects, landlords and tenants, learned and unlearned—all alike must carry arms and go to war. All have by nature a heart full of pride, unbelief, sloth, worldliness, and sin. All are living in a world beset with snares, traps, and pitfalls for the soul. All have near them a busy, restless, malicious devil. All, from the queen in her palace down to the pauper in the workhouse, all must fight, if they would be saved.

It is a fight of *perpetual necessity*. It admits of no breathing time, no armistice, no truce. On weekdays as well as on Sundays, in private as well as in public, at home by the family fireside as well as abroad, in little things like management of tongue and temper, as well as in great ones like the government of kingdoms, the Christian's warfare must unceasingly go on. The foe we have to do with keeps no holidays, never slumbers, and never sleeps. So long as we have breath in our bodies, we must keep on our armor and remember we are on an enemy's ground. "Even on the brink of Jordan," said a dying saint, "I find Satan nibbling at my heels." We must fight till we die.

Let us consider well these propositions. Let us take care that our own personal religion is real, genuine, and true. The saddest symptom about many so-called Christians is the utter absence of anything like conflict and fight in their Christianity. They eat, they drink, they dress, they work, they amuse themselves, they get money, they spend money, they go through a scanty round of formal religious services once or twice every week. But the great spiritual warfare—its watchings and strugglings, its agonies and anxieties, its battles and contests—of all this they appear to know nothing at all. Let us take care that this case is not our own. The worst state of soul is "when the strong man armed keepeth the house, and his goods are at peace," when he leads men and women "captive at his will," and they make no resistance. The worst chains are those that are neither felt nor seen by the prisoner. (Luke 11:21; 2 Tim. 2:26)

We may take comfort about our souls if we know anything of an inward fight and conflict. It is the invariable companion of genuine Christian holiness. It is not everything, I am well aware, but it is something. Do we find in our heart of hearts a spiritual struggle? Do we feel anything of the flesh lusting against the spirit and the spirit against the flesh, so that we cannot do the things we would (Gal. 5:17)? Are we conscious of two principles within us, contending for the mastery? Do we feel anything of war in our inward man? Well, let us thank God for it! It is a good sign. It is strongly probable evidence of the great work of sanctification. All true saints are soldiers. Anything is better than apathy, stagnation, deadness, and indifference. We are in a better state than many. The most part of so-called Christians have no feeling at all. We are evidently no friends of Satan. Like the kings of this world, he wars not against his own subjects. The very fact that he assaults us should fill our minds with hope. I say again, let us take comfort. The child of God has two great marks about him, and of these two we have one: He may be known by his *inward warfare*, as well as by his *inward peace*.

II

I pass on to the second thing that I have to say in handling my subject: true Christianity is the fight of faith. In this respect, the Christian warfare is utterly unlike the conflicts of this world. It does not depend on the strong arm, the quick eye, or the swift foot. It is not waged with carnal weapons, but with spiritual. Faith is the hinge on which victory turns. Success depends entirely on believing.

A general faith in the truth of God's written word is the primary foundation of the Christian soldier's character. He is what he is, does what he does, thinks as he thinks, acts as he acts, hopes as he hopes, behaves as he behaves, for one simple reason: he believes certain propositions revealed and laid down in Holy Scripture. "He that cometh to God must believe that He is, and that He is a Rewarder of them that diligently seek Him" (Heb. 11:6).

A religion without doctrine or dogma is a thing that many are fond of talking of in the present day. It sounds very fine at first. It looks very pretty at a distance. But the moment we sit down to examine and consider it, we shall find it a simple impossibility. We might as well talk of a body without bones and sinews. No man will ever be anything or do anything in religion unless he believes something. Even those who profess to hold the miserable and uncomfortable views of the deists are obliged to confess that they believe something. With all their bitter sneers against dogmatic theology and Christian credulity, as they call it, they themselves have a kind of faith.

As for true Christians, faith is the very backbone of their spiritual existence. No one ever fights earnestly against the world, the flesh, and the devil, unless he has engraven on his heart certain great principles that he believes. What they are he may hardly know, and may certainly not be able to define or write down. But there they are, and, consciously or unconsciously, they form the roots of his religion. Wherever you see a man, whether rich or poor, learned or unlearned, wrestling manfully with sin, and trying to overcome it, you may be sure there are certain great principles that that man believes. The poet who wrote the famous lines

For modes of faith let graceless zealots fight,
He can't be wrong whose life is in the right,

was a clever man, but a poor divine. There is no such thing as right living without faith and believing.

A special faith in our Lord Jesus Christ's person, work, and office is the life, heart, and mainspring of the Christian soldier's character.

He sees by faith an unseen Savior, who loved him, gave himself for him, paid his debts for him, bore his sins, carried his transgressions, rose again for him, and appears in heaven for him as his Advocate at the right hand of God. He sees Jesus and clings to him. Seeing this Savior and trusting in him, he feels peace and hope, and willingly does battle against the foes of his soul.

He sees his own many sins, his weak heart, a tempting world, a busy devil; and if he looked only at them, he might well despair. But he sees also a mighty Savior, an interceding Savior, a sympathizing Savior—his blood, his righteousness, his everlasting priesthood—and he believes that all this is his own. He sees Jesus and casts his whole weight on him. Seeing him, he cheerfully fights on, with a full confidence that he will prove "more than conqueror through Him that loved him" (Rom. 8:37).

Habitual lively faith in Christ's presence and readiness to help is the secret of the Christian soldier fighting successfully.

It must never be forgotten that faith admits of degrees. All men do not believe alike, and even the same person has his ebbs and flows of faith and believes more heartily at one time than another. According to the degree of his faith, the Christian fights well or ill, wins victories or suffers occasional repulses, comes off triumphant or loses a battle. He that has most faith will always be the happiest and most comfortable soldier. Nothing makes the anxieties of warfare sit so lightly on a man as the assurance of Christ's love and continual protection. Nothing enables him to bear the fatigue of watching, struggling, and wrestling against sin like the indwelling confidence that Christ is on his side and success is sure. It is the "shield of faith" that quenches all the fiery darts of the wicked one. It is the man who can say, "I know whom I have believed" who can say in time of suffering, "I am not ashamed."

He who wrote those glowing words, "We faint not," "Our light affliction which endureth but for a moment worketh in us a far more exceeding and eternal weight of glory" was the man who wrote with the same pen, "We look not at the things which are seen, but at the things which are not seen; for the things which are seen are temporal, but the things which are not seen are eternal." It is the man who said, "I live by the faith of the Son of God," who said, in the same epistle, "The world is crucified unto me, and I unto the world." It is the man who said, "To me to live is Christ," who said, in the same epistle, "I have learned in whatsoever state I am therewith to be content." "I can do all things through Christ." The more faith, the more victory! The more faith, the more inward peace! (Eph. 6:16; 2 Tim. 1:12; 2 Cor. 4:17, 18; Gal. 2:20; 6:14; Phil. 1:21; 4:11, 13)

I think it impossible to overrate the value and importance of faith. Well may the apostle Peter call it "precious" (2 Pet. 1:1). Time would fail me if I tried to recount a hundredth part of the victories that by faith Christian soldiers have obtained.

Let us take down our Bibles and read with attention the eleventh chapter of the epistle to the Hebrews. Let us mark the long list of worthies whose names are thus recorded, from Abel down to Moses, even before Christ was born of the Virgin Mary, and brought life and immortality into full light by the gospel. Let us note well what battles they won against the world, the flesh, and the devil. And then let us remember that believing did it all. These men looked forward to the promised Messiah. They saw him that is invisible. "By faith the elders obtained a good report" (Heb. 11:2–27).

Let us turn to the pages of early church history. Let us see how the primitive Christians held fast their religion even unto death and were not shaken by the fiercest persecutions of heathen emperors. For centuries, there were never wanting men like Polycarp and Ignatius, who were ready to die rather than deny Christ. Fines and prisons and torture and fire and sword were unable to crush the spirit of the noble army of martyrs. The whole power of imperial Rome, the mistress of the world, proved unable to stamp out the religion that began with a few fishermen and publicans in Palestine! And then let us remember that believing in an unseen Jesus was the church's strength. They won their victory by faith.

Let us examine the story of the Protestant Reformation. Let us study the lives of its leading champions—Wycliffe and Huss and Luther and Ridley and Latimer and Hooper. Let us mark how these gallant soldiers of Christ stood firm against a host of adversaries and were ready to die for their principles. What battles they fought! What controversies they maintained! What contradiction they endured! What tenacity of purpose they exhibited against a world in arms! And then let us remember that believing in an unseen Jesus was the secret of their strength. They overcame by faith.

Let us consider the men who have made the greatest marks in church history in the last hundred years. Let us observe how men like Wesley and Whitefield and Venn and Romaine stood alone in their day and generation, and revived English religion in the face of opposition from men high in office and in the face of slander, ridicule, and persecution from nine-tenths of professing Christians in our land. Let us observe how men like William Wilberforce and Havelock and Hedley Vicars have witnessed for Christ in the most difficult positions and displayed a banner for Christ even at the regimental mess table or on the floor of the House of Commons. Let us mark how these noble witnesses never flinched to the end and won the respect even of their worst adversaries. And then let us remember that believing in an unseen Christ is the key to all their characters. By faith they lived and walked and stood and overcame.

Would anyone live the life of a Christian soldier? Let him pray for faith. It is the gift of God and a gift that those who ask shall never ask for in vain. You must believe before you do. If men do nothing in religion, it is because they do not believe. Faith is the first step toward heaven.

Would anyone fight the fight of a Christian soldier successfully and prosperously? Let him pray for a continual increase of faith. Let him abide in Christ, get closer to Christ, tighten his hold on Christ every day that he lives. Let his daily prayer be that of the disciples: "Lord, increase my faith" (Luke 17:5). Watch jealously over your faith, if you have any. It is the citadel of the Christian character on which the safety of the whole fortress depends. It is the point that Satan loves to assail. All lies at his mercy if faith is overthrown. Here, if we love life, we must especially stand on our guard.

III

The last thing I have to say is this: true Christianity is a good fight.

"Good" is a curious word to apply to any warfare. All worldly war is more or less evil. No doubt, it is an absolute necessity in many cases—to procure the liberty of nations, to prevent the weak from being trampled down by the strong—but still it is an evil. It entails an awful amount of bloodshed and suffering. It hurries into eternity myriads who are completely unprepared for their change. It calls forth the worst passions of man. It causes enormous waste and destruction of property. It fills peaceful homes with mourning widows and orphans. It spreads far and wide poverty, taxation, and national distress. It disarranges all the order of society. It interrupts the work of the gospel and the growth of Christian missions. In short, war is an immense and incalculable evil, and every praying man should cry night and day, "Give peace in our time." And yet there is one warfare that is emphatically "good," and one fight in which there is no evil. That warfare is the Christian warfare. That fight is the fight of the soul.

Now what are the reasons why the Christian fight is a "good fight"? What are the points in which his warfare is superior to the warfare of this world? Let me examine this matter and open it out in order. I dare not pass the subject and leave it unnoticed. I want no one to begin the life of a Christian soldier without counting the cost. I would not keep back from anyone that if he would be holy and see the Lord he must fight, and that the Christian fight though spiritual is real and severe. It needs courage, boldness, and perseverance. But I want my readers to know that there is abundant encouragement, if they will only begin the battle.

The Scripture does not call the Christian fight "a good fight" without reason and cause. Let me try to show what I mean.

A. *The Christian's fight is good because it is under the best of generals.* The Leader and Commander of all believers is our divine Savior, the Lord Jesus Christ—a Savior of perfect wisdom, infinite love, and almighty power. The Captain of our salvation never fails to lead his soldiers to victory. He never makes any useless movements, never errs in judgment, never commits any mistake. His eye is on all his followers, from the greatest of them even to the least. The humblest servant in his army is not forgotten. The weakest and most sickly is cared for, remembered, and kept unto salvation. The souls whom he has purchased and redeemed with his own blood are far too precious to be wasted and thrown away. Surely this is good!

B. *The Christian's fight is good because it is fought with the best of helps.* Weak as each believer is in himself, the Holy Spirit dwells in him, and his body is a temple of the Holy Ghost. Chosen by God the Father, washed in the blood of the Son, renewed by the Spirit, he does not go a warfare at his own charges and is never alone. God the Holy Ghost daily teaches, leads, guides, and directs him. God the Father guards him by his almighty power. God the Son intercedes for him every moment, like Moses on the mount, while he is fighting in the valley below. A threefold cord like this can never be broken! His daily provisions and supplies never fail. His commissariat is never defective. His bread and his water are sure. Weak as he seems in himself, like a worm, he is strong in the Lord to do great exploits. Surely this is good!

C. The Christian fight is a good fight because it is fought with the best of promises. To every believer belong exceeding great and precious promises—all yes and amen in Christ—promises sure to be fulfilled because made by One who cannot lie and has power as well as will to keep his word. "Sin shall not have dominion over you." "The God of peace shall bruise Satan under your feet shortly." "He that has begun a good work will perform it until the day of Jesus Christ." "When thou passeth through the waters I will be with thee, and through the floods, they shall not overflow thee." "My sheep shall never perish, neither shall anyone pluck them out of my hand." "Him that cometh unto Me I will in no wise cast out." "I will never leave thee, nor forsake thee." "I am persuaded that neither death, nor life, nor things present, nor things to come, shall be able to separate us from the love of God, which is in Christ Jesus." (Rom. 6:14; Rom. 16:20; Phil. 1:6; Isa. 43:2; John 10:28; John 6:37; Heb. 13:5; Rom. 8:38)

Words like these are worth their weight in gold! Who does not know that promises of coming aid have cheered the defenders of besieged cities, like Lucknow, and raised them above their natural strength? Have we never heard that the promise of "help before night" had much to say to the mighty victory of Waterloo? Yet all such promises are as nothing compared to the rich treasure of believers, the eternal promises of God. Surely this is good!

D. *The Christian's fight is a good fight because it is fought with the best of issues and results.* No doubt, it is a war in which there are tremendous struggles, agonizing conflicts, wounds, bruises, watchings, fastings, and fatigue. But still, every believer, without exception, is "more than conqueror through Him that loved him" (Rom. 8:37). No soldiers of Christ are ever lost, missing, or left dead on the battlefield. No mourning will ever need to be put on, and no tears to be shed for either private or officer in the army of Christ. The muster roll, when the last evening comes, will be found precisely the same that it was in the morning. The English Guards marched out of London to the Crimean campaign a magnificent body of men; but many of the gallant fellows laid their bones in a foreign grave, and never saw London again. Far different shall be the arrival of the Christian army in "the city which hath foundations, whose builder and maker is God" (Heb. 11:10). Not one shall be found lacking. The words of our great Captain shall be found true: "Of them which thou hast given me I have lost none" (John 17:9). Surely this is good!

E. *The Christian's fight is good because it does good to the soul of him that fights it.* All other wars have a bad, lowering, and demoralizing tendency. They call forth the worst passions of the human mind. They harden the conscience and sap the foundations of religion and morality. The Christian warfare alone tends to call forth the best things that are left in man. It promotes humility and charity, it lessens selfishness and worldliness, it induces men to set their affections on things above. The old, the sick, the dying, are never known to repent of fighting Christ's battles against sin, the world, and the devil. Their only regret is that they did not begin to serve Christ long before. The experience of that eminent saint Philip Henry does not stand alone. In his last days, he said to his family, "I take you all to record that a life spent in the service of Christ is the happiest life that a man can spend upon earth." Surely this is good!

F. *The Christian's fight is a good fight because it does good to the world.* All other wars have a devastating, ravaging, and injurious effect. The march of an army through a land is an awful scourge to the inhabitants. Wherever it goes, it impoverishes, wastes, and does harm. Injury to persons, property, feelings, and morals invariably accompanies it. Far different are the effects produced by Christian soldiers. Wherever they live, they are a blessing. They raise the standard of religion and morality. They invariably check the progress of drunkenness, Sabbath-breaking, profligacy, and dishonesty. Even their enemies are obliged to respect them. Go where you please, you will rarely find that barracks and garrisons do good to the neighborhood. But go where you please, you will find that the presence of a few true Christians is a blessing. Surely this is good!

G. Finally, the Christian's fight is good because it ends in a glorious reward for all who fight it. Who can tell the wages that Christ will pay to all his faithful people? Who can estimate the good things that our divine Captain has laid up for those who confess him before men? A grateful country can give to her successful warriors medals, Victoria Crosses, pensions, peerages, honors, and titles. But it can give nothing that will last and endure for ever, nothing that can be carried beyond the grave. Palaces like Blenheim and Strathfieldsay can be enjoyed only for a few years. The bravest generals and soldiers must go down one day before the King of Terrors. Better, far better, is the position of him who fights under Christ's banner against sin, the world, and the devil. He may get little praise of man while he lives, and go down to the grave with little honor; but he shall have that which is far better, because far more enduring. He shall have "a crown of glory that fadeth not away" (1 Pet. 5:4). Surely this is good!

Let us settle it in our minds that the Christian fight is a good fight—really good, truly good, emphatically good. We see only part of it as yet. We see the struggle, but not the end; we see the campaign, but not the reward; we see the cross, but not the crown. We see a few humble, broken-spirited, penitent, praying people, enduring hardships and despised by the world; but we see not the hand of God over them, the face of God smiling on them, the kingdom of glory prepared for them. These things are yet to be revealed. Let us not judge by appearances.

There are more good things about the Christian warfare than we see.

IV

And now let me conclude my whole subject with a few words of practical application. Our lot is cast in times when the world seems thinking of little else but battles and fighting. The iron is entering into the soul of more than one nation, and the mirth of many a fair district is clean gone. Surely in times like these, a minister may fairly call on men to remember their spiritual warfare. Let me say a few parting words about the great fight of the soul.

It may be you are struggling hard for the rewards of this world. Perhaps you are straining every nerve to obtain money or place or power or pleasure. If that be your case, take care. Your sowing will lead to a crop of bitter disappointment. Unless you mind what you are about, your latter end will be to lie down in sorrow.

Thousands have trodden the path you are pursuing and have awoke too late to find it end in misery and eternal ruin. They have fought hard for wealth and honor and office and promotion and turned their backs on God and Christ and heaven and the world to come. And what has their end been? Often, far too often, they have found out that their whole life has been a grand mistake. They have tasted by bitter experience the feelings of the dying statesman who cried aloud in his last hours, "The battle is fought: the battle is fought: but the victory is not won."

For your own happiness's sake, resolve this day to join the Lord's side. Shake off your past carelessness and unbelief. Come out from the ways of a thoughtless, unreasoning world. Take up the cross, and become a good soldier of Christ. "Fight the good fight of faith," that you may be happy as well as safe.

Think what the children of this world will often do for liberty, without any religious principle. Remember how Greeks and Romans and Swiss and Tyrolese have endured the loss of all things, and even life itself, rather than bend their necks to a foreign yoke. Let their example provoke you to emulation. If men can do so much for a corruptible crown, how much more should you do for one that is incorruptible! Awake to a sense of the misery of being a slave. For life and happiness and liberty, arise and fight.

Fear not to begin and enlist under Christ's banner. The great Captain of your salvation rejects none that come to him. Like David in the cave of Adullam, he is ready to receive all who apply to him, however unworthy they may feel themselves. None who repent and believe are too bad to be enrolled in the ranks of Christ's army. All who come to him by faith are admitted, clothed, armed, trained, and finally led on to complete victory. Fear not to begin this very day. There is yet room for you.

Fear not to go on fighting, if you once enlist. The more thorough and wholehearted you are as a soldier, the more comfortable will you find your warfare. No doubt, you will often meet with trouble, fatigue, and hard fighting before your warfare is accomplished. But let none of these things move you. Greater is he that is for you than all they that be against you. Everlasting liberty or everlasting captivity are the alternatives before you. Choose liberty and fight to the last.

It may be you know something of the Christian warfare and are a tried and proved soldier already. If that be your case, accept a parting word of advice and encouragement from a fellow soldier. Let me speak to myself as well as to you. Let us stir up our minds by way of remembrance. There are some things that we cannot remember too well.

Let us remember that if we would fight successfully we must put on the whole armor of God, and never lay it aside till we die. Not a single piece of the armor can be dispensed with. The girdle of truth, the breastplate of righteousness, the shield of faith, the sword of the Spirit, the helmet of hope[1]—each and all are needful. Not a single day can we dispense with any part of this armor. Well says an old veteran in Christ's army, who died two hundred years ago, "In heaven we shall appear, not in armor, but in robes of glory. But here our arms are to be worn night and day. We must

---

[1] Most English translations of Eph. 6:17 have "helmet of salvation" instead of "helmet of hope."

walk, work, sleep in them, or else we are not true soldiers of Christ."[2]

Let us remember the solemn words of an inspired warrior, who went to his rest eighteen hundred years ago: "No man that warreth entangleth himself with the affairs of this life; that he may please him who hath chosen him to be a soldier" (2 Tim. 2:4). May we never forget that saying!

Let us remember that some have seemed good soldiers for a little season, and talked loudly of what they would do, and yet turned back disgracefully in the day of battle.

Let us never forget Balaam and Judas and Demas and Lot's wife. Whatever we are, and however weak, let us be real, genuine, true, and sincere.

2   William Gurnall, *The Christian in Complete Armour* (London: Blackie and Son, 1865), 64.

Let us remember that the eye of our loving Savior is upon us—morning, noon, and night. He will never suffer us to be tempted above that we are able to bear. He can be touched with the feeling of our infirmities, for he suffered himself being tempted. He knows what battles and conflicts are, for he himself was assaulted by the prince of this world. Having such a high priest, Jesus the Son of God, let us hold fast our profession (Heb. 4:14).

Let us remember that thousands of soldiers before us have fought the same battle that we are fighting, and come off more than conquerors through him that loved them. They overcame by the blood of the Lamb, and so also may we. Christ's arm is quite as strong as ever, and Christ's heart is just as loving as ever. He that saved men and women before us is one who never changes. He is "able to save to the uttermost all who come unto God by Him." Then let us cast doubts and fears away. Let us "follow them who through faith and patience inherit the promises," and are waiting for us to join them. (Heb. 7:25; 6:12)

Finally, let us remember that the time is short and the coming of the Lord draweth nigh. A few more battles and the last trumpet shall sound, and the Prince of Peace shall come to reign on a renewed earth. A few more struggles and conflicts, and then we shall bid an eternal goodbye to warfare and to sin, to sorrow, and to death. Then let us fight on to the last and never surrender. Thus saith the Captain of our salvation, "He that overcometh shall inherit all things; and I will be his God, and he shall be my son" (Rev. 21:7).

Let me conclude all with the words of John Bunyan, in one of the most beautiful parts of Pilgrim's Progress. He is describing the end of one of his best and holiest pilgrims:

After this it was noised abroad that Mr. Valiant-for-truth was sent for by a summons, by the same party as the others. And he had this word for a token that the summons was true, "The pitcher was broken at the fountain" (Eccles. 12:6). When he understood it, he called for his friends, and told them of it. Then said he, "I am going to my Father's house; and though with great difficulty I have got hither, yet now I do not repent me of all the troubles I have been at to arrive where I am. My sword I give to him that shall succeed me in my pilgrimage, and my courage and skill to him that can get it. My marks and scars I carry with me, to be a witness for me that I have fought His battles, who will now be my rewarder." When the day that he must go home was come, many accompanied him to the river-side, into which, as he went down, he said, "O death where is thy sting?" And as he went down deeper, he cried, "O grave, where is thy victory?" So he passed over, and all the trumpets sounded for him on the other side.[3]

May our end be like this! May we never forget that without fighting there can be no holiness while we live, and no crown of glory when we die!

3   John Bunyan, *The Pilgrim's Progress* (Québec: Samizdat, 2013), 269; full text available at http://www.samizdat.qc.ca/arts/lit /Pilgrims_Progress.pdf.

Scripture Index

Scripture Index

**CROSSWAY SHORT
CLASSICS**

Heaven Is a World of Love

Encouragement for the Depressed

The Expulsive Power of a New Affection

Fighting for Holiness

The Emotional Life of Our Lord

FOR MORE INFORMATION, VISIT **CROSSWAY.ORG**.